Endangered Animals

Written by Lucinda Hawksley
Illustrated by Michael Posen

p

This is a Parragon Publishing Book
This edition published in 2003

Parragon Publishing
Queen Street House
4 Queen Street
Bath BA1 1HE, UK

ISBN 0-75254-318-0

Printed in Dubai, UAE

Produced by
Monkey Puzzle Media Ltd

Designer: Sarah Crouch
Cover design: Victoria Webb
Editor: Linda Sonntag
Artwork commissioning:
Roger Goddard-Coote
Project manager: Alex Edmonds

Contents

How tall is a gorilla?

A FEMALE GORILLA STANDS AT ABOUT 4 FEET (1.2 metres) on her hind legs. A silverback male can reach up to 7 feet (2.1 metres), although the average height of a male is 5 feet 6 in (1.7 metres). Males are called "silverbacks" when hair on their backs turns silver in mature adulthood.

Silverback gorilla

Gorillas are the most intelligent animals next to human beings.

What do gorillas need from their habitat?
Shelter and a good supply of food. If the climate is favorable, both mountain and lowland habitats can provide a gorilla family with all the food and nutrients they need. Mountain gorillas are severely endangered. Gorillas are mainly vegetarian and their habitats are rich in lush vegetation, as well as plentiful insects.

How do gorillas communicate?
They use body signals and noises – perhaps the most famous of these is the male's habit of standing on his hind legs and beating his chest when angry. They play together, which teaches their young vital skills for survival.

What happens to gorillas in wartime?
Gorillas are often innocent victims of fierce fighting. Occasionally, they get caught in the crossfire. Hungry troops may also track down a gorilla and kill it for food. As there are very few gorillas left in the world, killing even one could contribute to the extinction of the species.

Are we related to gorillas?

Yes. Gorillas and humans have a common ancestor. This creature lived on earth many millions of years ago. The descendants of our common ancestor started two separate families, or evolutionary lines. One became human, the other became the ancestor of gorillas. Like humans, gorillas are a member of the Primate order. Within this order, both humans, and gorillas are members of a scientific family called *Hominoidea*.

Why are gorillas hunted?

Tragically, one of the most common reasons they are hunted is as 'trophies' – so hunters can show off their skills. Gorillas' skulls, hands, and feet are sold as souvenirs, just as elephant feet were in the 19th century. Gorillas have also been hunted for their meat, particularly during the famine that gripped Rwanda in the 1980s and 1990s.

What is life like in the gorilla group?

Gorilla society is run by male gorillas – it is called a patriarchal society, from the Latin word for father. The leader of the group is always a silverback (a mature male). Males often fight to show who is the boss, and the loser must leave the group, or be killed. Those that leave will often set up a new group of females and young.

Can people see gorillas in the wild?

Yes, small groups of people are taken to the gorillas' habitat. There are strict rules and people have to be extremely careful not to disturb the gorillas. Visitors are kept at a respectful distance and instructed how to behave. Human illnesses – even the common cold – can be caught by gorillas and could prove fatal, because they have no resistance to our diseases. So people should not attempt the trip if they feel at all unwell.

Who tried to save the gorillas?

Dr Dian Fossey was the gorillas' most famous helper. She spent much of her life trying to stop gorillas being captured or killed for trade. Sadly she was murdered in 1985. Since Dian Fossey's death, many action groups have continued her work. The story of her life was made into a film, *Gorillas In The Mist*.

Why are gorillas endangered?

GORILLAS LIVE IN AFRICA – IN ZAIRE, RWANDA, AND UGANDA – IN mountainous areas, and in the lowland rainforests. In 1925, their mountain home was made the first national park in Africa. Sadly, Zaire, Rwanda, and Uganda have suffered severely over the last few decades, experiencing terrifying wars, droughts, and famines. This has caused terrible devastation to the gorilla population, as well as to the human world. All gorilla species are endangered.

Mountain gorilla

The mountain gorilla is the most endangered of the gorillas.

5

Most colobus monkeys have a shortened – or missing – thumb.

Colobus monkey

Which species of monkey are in danger?

T HE MOST ENDANGERED SPECIES IS THE gorilla. Orangutans are also at risk from poachers, but more at risk is Africa's colobus monkey, which is often killed for its luxuriant black-and-white coat. India's lion-tailed macaque is also at risk from poachers and from erosion of its habitat.

Where do monkeys come from?
Monkeys can be found in Asia, Africa, and Central and South America. They prefer warm climates, although a few species live in cold areas, such as the Himalayas. Most types of monkey live in areas where trees are plentiful, although some African monkeys live in the savannah (grassland) with few trees.

How many types of monkey are there?
There are around 133 different species of monkey in the world. Monkeys are primates – a type of mammal. Other primates include humans, bushbabies, lemurs and marmosets. Many marmosets are endangered. A collective term for monkeys is anthropoids. This word means that they share similarities with human beings.

6

How do baby monkeys climb trees?

Baby monkeys cling on to their mother's fur and swing through the trees with her. Some species carry their young on their backs, some underneath their bellies, like a kangaroo – only without a protective pouch. Baby monkeys have to cling on with the tightest grip imaginable to survive the rigorous journeys.

Which religion has a monkey god?

Hinduism. The monkey god's name is Hanuman and his mischievous sense of humour often gets him into trouble. He plays an important part in one of Hinduism's scriptures, the Ramayana. In one story he helps Rama rescue his kidnapped wife, Sita. At holy festivals, Hindu men sometimes dress up as Hanuman.

Can monkeys talk?

Monkeys don't talk like humans do, but they do have their own highly developed languages. Howler monkeys shout very loudly to one another. When monkeys talk together in a group they sound very excited, and the noise is often referred to as chattering. People who study the way monkeys communicate believe they can discuss plans for moving to new feeding grounds.

How big is a monkey?

Monkeys range vastly in size. The smallest is the tiny pygmy marmoset, which weighs approximately 5 oz (150 g); the largest is the mountain gorilla – males can stand up to 7 feet (2.1 metres) tall and weigh over 500 lb (225 kg). There are monkeys of all sizes in between these extremes.

What do monkeys eat?

Monkeys eat fruit, leaves, nuts, plants, insects and small animals. They will also drink water, although as their diet is rich in moisture, they often don't need to drink as well as eat. Most monkeys spend much of their life in trees, which is where they find their food.

Pygmy marmoset

The pygmy marmoset likes to gnaw holes in trees and feed on the gum that oozes out.

Have any species become extinct?

NOT IN RECENT CENTURIES. CHINA'S YUNNAN SNUB-NOSED MONKEY was believed to be extinct because it had not been spotted for 70 years. But recently it was rediscovered – the population numbers around 1,000. Brazil's golden lion tamarins were on the brink of extinction. But thanks to the work of conservation groups such as WWF, their numbers are now increasing.

Which red wolf may not be around much longer?

The red wolf in the USA has been cross-bred with so many other species that it is now endangered.

Are there wolves in Australia?

Yes, but maybe not for long. The Tasmanian wolf used to live happily in Australia, but conservationists haven't spotted one for well over ten years, so they are beginning to become concerned that it has been hunted to extinction.

Are pet dogs endangered?

No! The ancestors of all domestic dogs were once wild animals. They were tamed by people who found them useful for hunting and as guards for their property. Today, after many centuries of domestication, most pet dogs are totally different from their wild ancestors – and not endangered at all.

What bones are used in folk medicine?

CONSERVATIONISTS ARE TRYING TO STOP canines being killed for their fur, and for parts of their bodies used in traditional medicines. In Africa, the simien jackal is hunted for its beautiful coat, and in South America the maned wolf is hunted for its bones. When powdered, the bones are believed to cure a variety of ills.

Does a fox cub make a good pet?

No wild animal should be kept as a pet. It takes many generations of breeding to completely tame any species. A fox cub may seem very playful and friendly, but its wild instincts would soon take over. No other pets, such as cats or rabbits, would be safe from it, and it could also attack humans, even those it knew well, through fear.

Jackals like to feed on fruit, small mammals and even the bodies of larger animals that have died.

Simien jackal

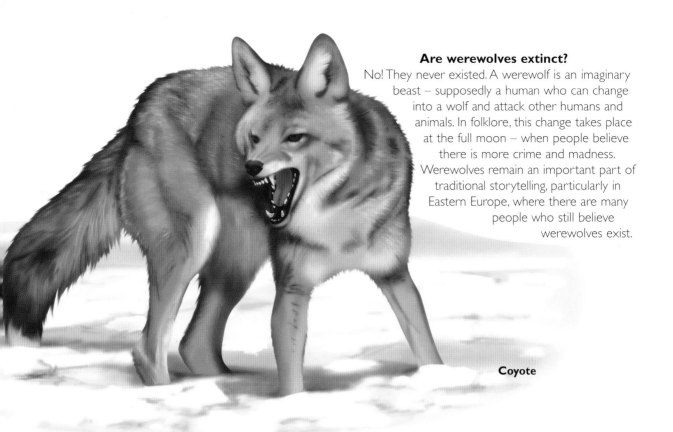

Are werewolves extinct?
No! They never existed. A werewolf is an imaginary beast – supposedly a human who can change into a wolf and attack other humans and animals. In folklore, this change takes place at the full moon – when people believe there is more crime and madness. Werewolves remain an important part of traditional storytelling, particularly in Eastern Europe, where there are many people who still believe werewolves exist.

Coyote

A coyote's howl can be heard several miles away.

Which is the smallest wild dog?
The smallest alive today is the fennec fox, which lives in parts of Africa and the Middle East. The fennec fox is under threat from predators and habitat erosion. When born, a fennec cub weighs only 2 lb (0.8 kg); as an adult it will weigh about 3 lb (1.5 kg). The largest wild dog of all is the gray wolf – an adult can weigh up to 176 lb (80 kg).

When did wolves become extinct in Britain?
Once Britain was almost covered in dense forest. When people began cutting it down, they destroyed the wolves' habitat and source of food – making wolves hungry and dangerous. The last wolf killed in Britain was in Scotland, in 1743. Ireland's last wolf perished about 50 years before, and in England, wolves were extinct by 1500.

In what countries do wolves, foxes, and wild dogs live?

I**N EVERY CONTINENT. THERE ARE WOLVES IN EASTERN EUROPE AND ASIA,** jackals in Africa, coyotes in America, and dingoes in Australia. From the black-backed jackal in Africa to the gray wolf in Europe, many wolves are under threat. The wolves hunt in packs and kill their own prey as well as scavenging on dead animals. All wolves are disliked by farmers!

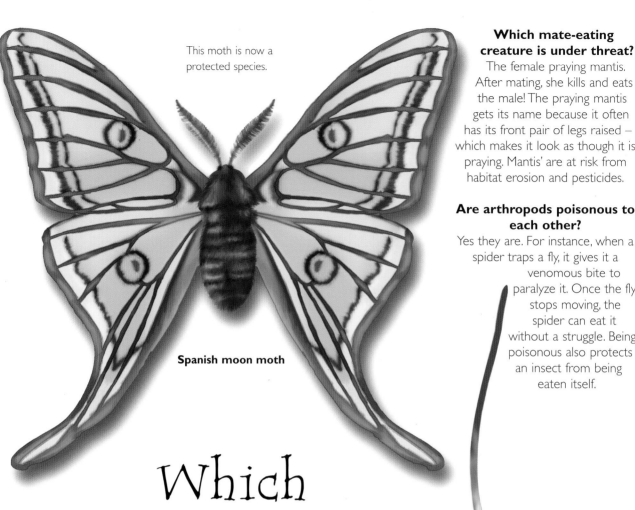

This moth is now a protected species.

Spanish moon moth

Which mate-eating creature is under threat?
The female praying mantis. After mating, she kills and eats the male! The praying mantis gets its name because it often has its front pair of legs raised – which makes it look as though it is praying. Mantis' are at risk from habitat erosion and pesticides.

Are arthropods poisonous to each other?
Yes they are. For instance, when a spider traps a fly, it gives it a venomous bite to paralyze it. Once the fly stops moving, the spider can eat it without a struggle. Being poisonous also protects an insect from being eaten itself.

Which insects have become extinct?

Today, arthropods (insects and arachnids) make up 80 per cent of all animal species on earth. And because fossillized remains have been found, we know that many hundreds of species have also become extinct in the past. More recently, the Duke of Burgundy butterfly, from Europe, and the American burying beetle. from the USA, are just two of many insects that have become extinct. The Spanish moon moth and giant weta cricket are at risk and are now protected species. Scientists think that there are many more living arthropods still to be discovered, and probably more extinct species, too.

How can you tell an arachnid from an insect?

The most obvious difference is in the number of legs. An insect (for example, an ant) has six legs, and an arachnid (for example, a scorpion) has eight. Both insects and arachnids are members of a large group called arthropods. This group also includes crustaceans (such as crabs), centipedes, and millipedes. Many arthropods are endangered by human activities.

Why are people scared of spiders?

Many people are frightened of spiders because of the unusual way they move. A fear of spiders (called arachnophobia, from the Latin words for spiders and fear) is one of the most common phobias in the world. Really, spiders should be afraid of humans because many of them, such as the bone cave harvestman, and the spruce-fir moss spider from the USA, are endangered.

Which insects and arachnids are poisonous?

MORE THAN YOU MIGHT THINK! SCORPIONS AND REDBACK SPIDERS are well known to be poisonous. But in fact most insects are poisonous to a greater or lesser degree. A wasp sting is poisonous, and hurts, but in large doses (or to those who are allergic) it can be fatal. Most spider venom would be poisonous to humans — but very few spiders are able to bite through human skin. If they can, most inject only a small dose of venom.

What creature could survive a nuclear war?

There are many endangered arthropods, such as the painted rocksnail from the USA. Many live in the rainforests. Their habitat is being destroyed at an alarming rate, making countless arthropod species extinct each year. However, they are also extremely hardy — scientists believe cockroaches would be the only creatures to survive a nuclear war!

Which beach-dwelling arthropods are at risk?

Many arthropods live in beach or ocean habitats. They are under threat from pollution, which makes the beach and water uninhabitable. Many crab, shrimp, and crayfish species are at risk, such as the longhorn fairy shrimp and the common cave crayfish, both from the USA. Arthropods are also killed in huge numbers by pesticides, and many are lost when their wild habitat is destroyed for building.

Giant weta cricket

Fossilized weta crickets have been found that date back more than 180 million years ago.

Which snail was eaten to extinction?

All seven species of land snail were once found in Moorea, in French Polynesia. When French settlers imported their own French snails to farm for eating, these larger foreign visitors ate the local snails and they no longer exist!

The red panda eats bamboo, roots and some small animals.

Red panda

How many types of panda are there?

THE GIANT PANDA HAS ONE OTHER panda relation – the red panda. Red pandas are much smaller, and used to be thought of as not a panda at all, but a type of raccoon. They live in trees, have long, striped tails and thin, cat-like faces with pointed ears. Their red fur has paler markings. Red pandas are often hunted, and some are captured alive, to be sold as pets.

Where do giant pandas live?

In bamboo forests in China. Once they were seen all over this vast country, but sadly today they can be found in only three small provinces in western China.

Red pandas are more adaptable to changes in habitat, and can be found in China and other parts of Asia, including the Himalayas.

Which animal is all thumbs?

Giant pandas have an extra "finger" on their front paws. It is where a human's little finger would be, and works like a thumb. This gives the panda the power of two thumbs, so it can grip its food while eating.

Are pandas vegetarian?

Like all bears, pandas are omnivorous, which means they eat meat or vegetation. But giant pandas seldom eat meat, for the simple reason that they find it difficult to catch! If they come across a dead or wounded animal they will eat it, but they usually eat vegetation, and almost always this is bamboo.

How many giant pandas are left in the world?

There are believed to be fewer than 1,000 giant pandas left in the wild. Since 1974 their bamboo forests have died out at an alarming rate: in just 14 years half the forests died. Since then conservationists have been working tirelessly to preserve the pandas' habitat.

How long does a panda take to eat lunch?

Almost all its waking hours! Giant pandas spend around 14 hours every day eating. An adult panda will eat up to 66 lb (30 kg) of bamboo in a day – this is one third of its body weight! The reason they need to eat so much is because bamboo has very little nutritional value.

How often do giant pandas have babies?

Their cubs are born only every two years, at the most. This is another reason why giant pandas are endangered, especially as many cubs die shortly after birth. Cubs are born blind, and without teeth, making them entirely dependent on their mothers.

What is threatening the Giant Panda?

THE SHORTAGE OF BAMBOO, WHICH IS THE PANDA'S FOOD. BAMBOO FORESTS ARE very delicate. Bamboo does not keep growing like other forest plants. When it flowers, it dies. If the bamboo in one forest is all of the same age, the whole forest will die at the same time. All the pandas living in that forest will then starve. Humans are the pandas' biggest enemies, because they have taken their land and hunted them. It is now illegal in China to harm a panda in any way, and traders risk the death penalty.

How much do giant pandas weigh?

Around 19 stone (120 kg). They have heavy bones and thick fur. It is this beautiful fur that has led to many giant pandas being slaughtered by hunters.

Giant panda

The giant panda has special cheek teeth for crushing and slicing plant food.

Bears have bad eyesight, so tend to hunt their prey by smell.

Do bears really like honey?
Yes they do. Many bears are expert climbers, and with their excellent sense of smell, finding a bee's nest is easy for them. Bears are omnivorous, which means they eat both meat and vegetation. They like eating other mammals, insects (even wasps, bees and termites, whose stings seem not to bother them), plants, nuts, fish, eggs, fruit, and people's picnics – if they can find them. They will also eat carrion (rotting meat) if necessary.

Spectacled bear

When is a brown bear blue?

Not counting pandas, there are seven species of bear: the American black bear, Asian black bear, brown bear, polar bear, sloth bear, spectacled bear, and sun bear. These names are very misleading. For instance, a brown bear's coat can range in color from cream to very dark brown, and it can also look gray-blue! Black bears can also be brown and, to most people who aren't experts, two bears of the same species can look very different from one another.

Are polar bears endangered?
Polar bears live in the Arctic, the area around the North Pole. The other species of bear are found all over North and South America, parts of Europe, and Asia. They live in the mountains and lowland, in areas where food is plentiful, but they are endangered by hunters, who are after polar bear skin and meat.

Why should a bear follow its nose?
Bears often have bad eyesight, which is made up for by an excellent sense of smell. This sense is vital to the survival of the species. It warns them of danger, in the form of humans, or other predatory animals, and tells them where to find water and food.

Why are bears hunted?

For their bones, bile, and gall bladders, which are made into traditional medicines, and for their fur. Bear meat is also eaten, in particular their paws. And there are still people who hunt bears as "trophies" for sport. Most cruelly, bears are trapped to be used as dancing bears or for bear baiting.

Why do bears hibernate?

They sleep all winter because food is scarce. In summer a bear will eat continually, storing up fat to use for energy during the winter. Females need to store up very large fat reserves as their cubs are born during hibernation, and need to be fed with rich milk.

Why is a grizzly bear grizzly?

A grizzly is actually one of the many different types of brown bear. The word grizzly comes from the french word *gris*, meaning gray. When the sun catches a grizzly bear's fur, the tips of the hairs look as if they are tinged with gray.

Grizzlies are solitary animals, apart from the springtime, when males search for females to mate with.

The kodiak bear is a type of grizzly bear.

Kodiak bear

Do bears like fish?

Yes, fish makes up a large part of their diet in parts of the world where rivers are plentiful. In North America, Alaska, and Canada bears can often be seen skilfully catching enormous salmon.

Which is the biggest bear?

The biggest bear in the world is the endangered Kodiak bear, a member of the brown bear species. It lives in Alaska and stands up to 10 feet (3 m) tall. It can weigh up to 704 lb (320 kg).

Grizzly bear

Which bears are most endangered?

The most endangered bear in the world is the giant panda, although all species of brown bear, the polar bear, and black bears are killed for their fur, and are under threat from fur hunters.

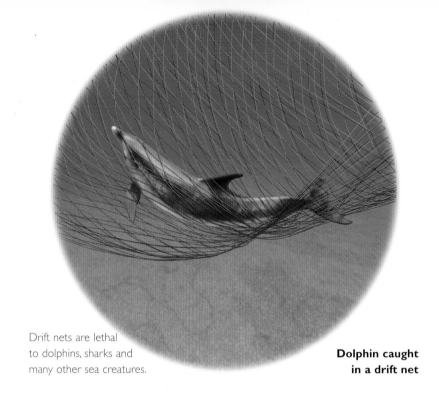

Drift nets are lethal
to dolphins, sharks and
many other sea creatures.

**Dolphin caught
in a drift net**

What is a cetacean?

Cetacean is the word for all
species of whale, dolphin, and
porpoise. There are about 80
different species of cetacean and
many, including the Indus and
Ganges river dolphins, the
southern right whale, and the
beluga whale, are endangered. The
first cetaceans lived on land,
around 60 million years ago. Today
they live in seas, oceans, and some
rivers all over the world – but they
are mammals, not fish.

What is the difference between a dolphin and a porpoise?

They are quite hard to tell apart
without examining their teeth!
Dolphins have teeth shaped like
cones, but porpoise's teeth are
spade-shaped. Porpoises are usually
smaller than dolphins, and have
more rounded bellies. The two
groups often swim together and are
extremely playful. There are
endangered species within both
groups, such as the vaquita
porpoise and the Yangtze
river dolphin.

How do drift nets kill dolphins and sharks?

Drift nets are enormous nets used for commercial fishing. They cover huge
areas, often reaching right down to the sea-bed. The nets trap and kill many
other sea creatures, as well as fish – especially dolphins, porpoises, sharks, and
turtles. Drift nets have been banned in most countries, but are still used illegally.

Why must we save the whales?

The ecosystem of the seas is very delicate. Breaking one link in the food
chain, that goes all the way from the smallest microscopic creature to the
biggest whale, would have devastating effects. In 1986, the International
Whaling Commission (IWC) announced a worldwide ban on whaling.
Today it allows a small number of whales to be taken every year "for
scientific reasons." Peoples, like the Inuit, who have always depended
on whaling, are allowed to continue whaling using
traditional methods.

Are killer whales killers?

NO. A KILLER WHALE, OR ORCA, IS UNLIKELY TO EAT A PERSON.

They prefer to eat fish, other cetaceans, and seals. In fact they are in more danger from humans than vice versa. In New Zealand an orca once tried to eat a man diving near a colony of seals. The man was wearing a shiny black wetsuit and must have looked like a sleek, tasty sea lion. When the orca realized its mistake it spat the man out and he survived!

How big is the biggest whale?

The biggest whale is the blue whale which is now officially protected to prevent its extinction. It is the largest-known mammal ever to have lived. The average length of a female is 87 feet (26.2 m); males are shorter at about 80 feet (24.1 m). The biggest recorded blue whale measured 110 feet (33 m) and weighed 160 tons.

What happens to cetaceans when people catch too many fish?

If there are not enough fish, cetaceans will starve. The more fish that are caught, the more cetaceans die. Fishermen also sometimes kill cetaceans, to stop them "stealing" their catch. Of course, overfishing is not good for fish either. It affects how the ones that are left behind reproduce and where they breed.

If too many fish are caught, the world's fish stocks could slowly die out. Cetaceans would die with them.

Which whale has a horn like a unicorn?

The narwhal, which lives in waters around the Arctic, is almost extinct. The male narwhal has a horn or tusk, which is actually a very long tooth, made of ivory. Very occasionally a narwhal has two tusks. The myth of unicorns probably began when an explorer returned to Europe with a narwhal's tusk.

A sperm whale can swim over half a mile (1 km) below the surface of the sea and hold its breath for around one hour.

Sperm whale

How do whales eat?

ALL DOLPHINS AND PORPOISES, AND SOME WHALES,

have teeth. Other whales, such as the almost extinct blue whale, have baleen – this is a huge sieve, made up of hundreds of stiff blades of keratin, a type of protein like fingernails. Baleen whales sieve the microscopic shrimp-like creatures, called krill, with these tools. Toothed cetaceans, such as the endangered sperm whale, eat fish and sea creatures, such as seals, squid, and smaller cetaceans.

What sea cow is about to die out?

Sea cow is the name for both manatees and dugongs, the two remaining members of the order *Sirenia*. They were nicknamed sea cows because they graze plants that grow on the sea-bed, just as cows graze in fields. Both of these animals are so badly endangered that they are expected to be extinct by around 2020.

Are sharks related to whales?

No, a shark is a fish, and a whale is a mammal – fish are cold-blooded, and mammals are warm-blooded. The best way to tell if you are looking at a whale or a shark is that the point of a shark's tail sticks up out of the water, but a whale's tail lies flat against the surface. Whales need air to breathe, which they do through blowholes on the top of their heads, but sharks do not need air to breathe, and have gills. Hammerhead sharks, great white sharks, and the Ganges shark are just three of the long list of endangered sharks.

What sea creatures are in danger?

ENDANGERED SEA CREATURES INCLUDE MANATEES, dugongs, and some turtles, seals, sharks, cetaceans, and coral (which is an animal and not a plant, as is often believed). Many creatures that live in the Mediterranean Sea, such as the green sea turtle and monk seal, are also endangered because it is the most polluted sea on earth.

Manatees like to rest on the bottom of the ocean on their backs – as if they were sunbathing!

Did mermaids become extinct?

No! They never existed. Unlikely as it may sound, the myth of mermaids came from delirious sailors seeing sea cows! Manatees and dugongs sing in a rasping, grunting way, and sometimes sailors, suffering from a lack of food and water, mistook them for beautiful women singing with harmonious voices.

Are sea snakes poisonous?

Yes, a bite from a sea snake can kill a healthy adult in five minutes. However, unlike land snakes, sea snakes cannot dislocate their jaws, which means they usually can't open their mouths wide enough to bite you. Sea snakes are at risk of extinction, where there is pollution, and where coral reefs are breaking down due to habitat erosion.

Is the sea-horse really a horse?

Sea-horse

No, A SEA-HORSE IS A FISH. ITS NAME COMES FROM ITS LONG, CURVED neck and head, which are shaped like a horse's. Sea-horses also swim upright, like herds of miniature horses prancing on their hind legs. Centuries ago people believed that sea-horses could grow as big as real horses, but in fact they are small, fragile creatures.

Sea-horses are so bad at adapting to changes in their environment that they are now in danger of extinction.

Why is the monk seal dying out?

The monk seal, a gray seal that lives around the Mediterranean, was once a common sight, but no longer. Fishermen kill these seals because they don't like them eating "their" fish. Many other sea creatures have become endangered for the same reason.

Can a plastic bag kill a sea creature?

Yes, quite easily. Humans pollute the seas with oil and fuel spills, with sewage, and harmful chemicals. People also kill sea creatures by driving boats and jet-skis recklessly or by leaving rubbish. A plastic bag floating in the water looks like a jellyfish, but any animal that swallows it, such as a turtle, will die.

Manatee

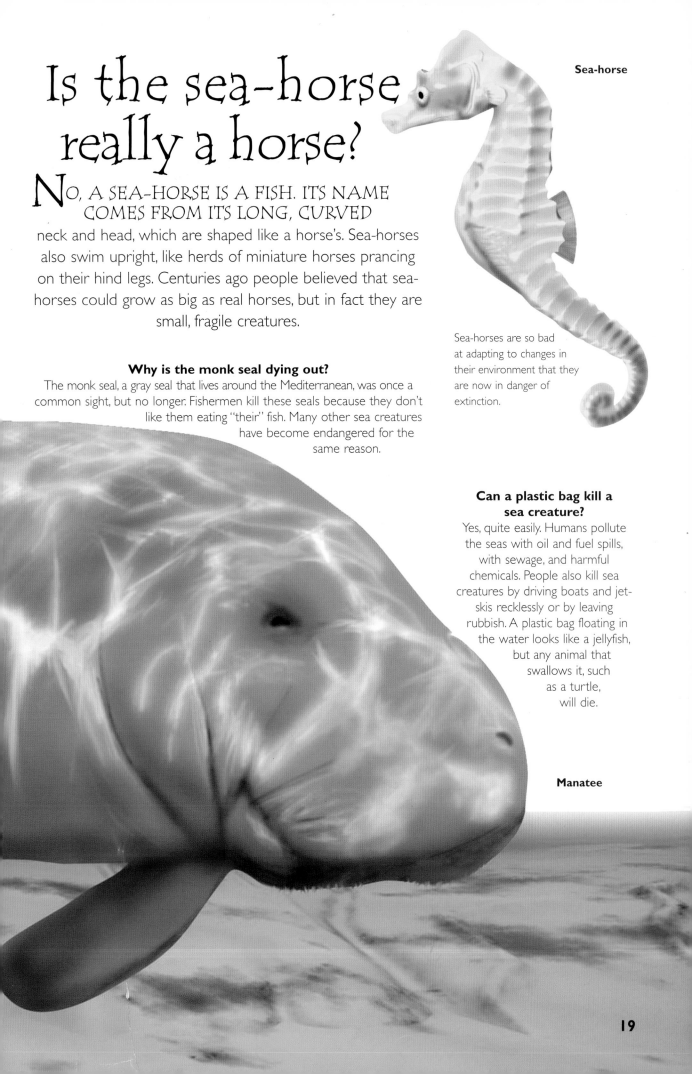

Javan rhinoceros

Rhinos have a very good sense of smell and good hearing.

Why are rhinos in danger of extinction?

Because there are so few rhinos left in the world, that just a few more years of hunting could wipe them out. An added danger is the sinister fact that, when something is in short supply, it always becomes more valuable – some poachers want to kill all rhinos just to make the rhino horn they own even more valuable.

Where does the rhinoceros get its name?

Rhino means nose, and ceros means horn – the dinosaur *Triceratops* was so-named because it had three horns. A rhinoceros's horn is a useful weapon in a fight, and scares off many predators. Horns are made of a protein called keratin (like human hair and nails), which is very hard.

Why are rhinos killed?

Unfortunately, rhinos are hunted for their horns, which many peoples believe have magical or medicinal powers. Traditional herbalists give powdered rhino horn to people suffering from fever and for use in love potions. In North Yemen rhino horns are carved to make dagger handles.

Where do rhinos live?

White and black rhinos live all over Africa. The Javan, Sumatran, and Indian rhinos, as their names suggest, live in Java, Sumatra, and India, all countries in Asia. Rhinos are also kept in zoos and safari parks all over the world. Many wildlife sanctuaries have set up rhinoceros breeding programmes, hoping to help save the species from extinction.

How many rhinos are there left in the world?

There are less than 8,500 white rhinos still living. Almost all of these are southern whites, so the northern white rhinos are extremely endangered. There are around 2,600 black rhinos; 2,050 Indian rhinos; about 400 Sumatran rhinos; and – most endangered of all – only around 70 Javan rhinos left.

What is the rhino's biggest enemy?

Big cats prey on rhinos, but they kill only a few. Humans are the reason rhinos are endangered. As well as poachers wanting their horn, farmers often shoot rhinos to stop them eating or trampling their crops. Previously, rhinos were also shot as "trophies" by big-game hunters.

Black rhinoceros

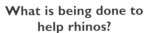

What is being done to help rhinos?

Where rhinos are found there are also specially trained guards. Obviously they can't be with the animals all the time, but they track them and make sure they know where the groups are. In many parts of the world, conservationists tranquilize rhinos and saw off their horns. This is not painful – it is like us cutting our hair or nails. Conservationists hope that if a rhino has no horn, the poachers will not kill it.

Does the rhino have any extinct relations?

THERE ARE FIVE SPECIES OF RHINO: WHITE, BLACK, SUMATRAN, JAVAN, and Indian and they are all endangered. Thousands and thousands of years ago the rhino had a great many more relations – there was even a woolly rhino, with a similar coat to the woolly mammoth – but these are all now extinct.

The black rhinoceros has no hair on its body and a very thick skin or hide.

What is happening to the rhinos' habitat?

Many Asian rhinos are endangered because their habitat – the rainforest – has been cut down for timber. This is a worldwide problem, as most rainforest countries are also poor countries, that need to sell their resources. In Africa, the savannah (grassland), where the rhinos live, is often under threat of drought.

Where do elephants live?

AS THEIR NAMES SUGGEST, AFRICAN ELEPHANTS LIVE IN AFRICA – IN countries such as Kenya, Zimbabwe, South Africa, and Tanzania. Asian elephants live, of course, in Asia – in Nepal, India, Sri Lanka, and Thailand. Both species are able to survive, in either tropical forests, or savannah (grassland) areas.

African elephants are larger than Asian elephants.

Which elephant ancestor became extinct 11,000 years ago?
In the past there were many species of elephant and their relatives. One was the woolly mammoth, which died out about 11,000 years ago. Its coat was so warm, it lived as far north as Britain. Today the elephants' closest relation is a small mammal, the hyrax, which is the size of a little dog!

How do elephants communicate?
To warn of danger – perhaps hunters after ivory – elephants make a trumpeting sound. They are very affectionate creatures and often walk along with their trunks touching another member of the group – mothers and their babies especially.

What happens to elephants in captivity?
Male elephants can become very aggressive, which is how they react in the wild, if threatened. Wild elephants cover enormous distances in a single day's walking, so keeping them in an enclosure – even one that seems big to us – can make an elephant extremely unhappy. The stress they suffer can shorten their lifespan and affect breeding.

How heavy is a baby elephant?
At birth, baby Asian elephants weigh about 440 lb (200 kg); baby African elephants are heavier, at around 581 lb (264 kg). This may seem very heavy, but the babies have a long way to go to reach the average adult weight of 4 tons.

Can elephants cry?
Many people, who know elephants well, are sure that they do cry. Zoologists often say that elephants' tears have nothing to do with sadness, but people have often seen elephants cry when they find a dead elephant. Others report that circus elephants cry when they are cruelly treated.

African elephant

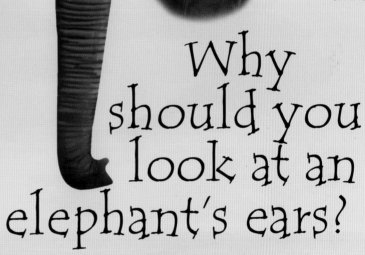

Why do people kill elephants?

Some people kill them because they threaten their homes and crops; but more often they are killed for their tusks, which are made of ivory. Ivory was used in the past for making white chess pieces, carved ornaments, piano keys, and even false teeth! Today it is against international law to sell ivory, but many traders still manage to make a fortune from selling it illegally.

African elephant

Asian elephant

The ears of an African elephant are a similar shape to the continent of Africa.

Asian elephants are often dressed in colorful materials to take part in Indian ceremonies.

What can be done to save the elephants?

The ban on selling ivory needs to be enforced, so that poachers and traders can be caught and punished. The elephants' habitat also needs to be protected. In recent years, conservationists have begun to study new ways of coping with elephants as neighbors. And electronic tracking devices have been fixed to high-risk elephants, so that rangers can monitor them.

Why should you look at an elephant's ears?

THERE ARE TWO SPECIES OF ELEPHANT: THE ASIAN ELEPHANT AND THE

African elephant, and both are endangered. The easiest way to tell them apart is by their ears — those of an Asian elephant are smaller. It is sometimes said that the ears of an African elephant are a similar shape to the continent of Africa. Another difference between the two is their tusks: both male and female African elephants have tusks; whereas only male Asian elephants have them (and these are sometimes very small).

What is the elephant's worst enemy?

People. Healthy elephants have no natural predators, apart from humans — their weight, strength, and habit of living in large herds protect them from packs of hunting animals. The herd will usually stay with a wounded elephant, keeping away scavengers such as big cats. Baby elephants are equally fiercely protected.

23

The iriomote looks very similar to a domestic cat.

Iriomote cat

Which big cats are endangered?

MANY BIG CATS ARE ENDANGERED BY HUNTERS, BECAUSE OF THE BEAUTY of their skin. Hunters can get rich selling the pelts (skins) of slaughtered big cats (such as the ocelot), to people who make fur coats. Some hunters still kill big cats for sport. Many big cats, such as the mountain lion, are also threatened with the loss of their habitat, which is destroyed by developers, or by wars. The most endangered big cats are: mountain lion, tiger, snow leopard (also called an ounce), jaguar, ocelot, clouded leopard, iriomote, and cheetah.

Are big cats related to domestic cats?

Yes, they are. All cats are of the order *Carnivora* (meat-eaters) and the family *Felidae* (felines). The domestic cat has much in common with the tiger, and its large relations. They hunt in similar ways and they all eat meat, but unlike their relations, they are not endangered.

Do lions climb trees to escape danger?

No. They often climb trees to look out over the surrounding land, to search for prey and to sleep, protected from the sun. Lions will not climb trees after a big meal, as they eat so much at one time that they need several hours to digest their prey.

What is big and lazy?

The male lion is the biggest of the cat family, weighing about 528 lb (240 kg). Despite his size, he does little work, leaving the hunting and killing of his food, and the raising of cubs, to the lioness. Lions can sleep for up to 20 hours a day. All lions are on the list of endangered animals.

Tigers are unusual cats because they like water.

Tiger

Do big cats mate for life?
No. A male cat may have more than one mate at a time, and females may mate with a different male, from one season to the next. Males live alone or with one or more females. They can't live together, as they fight over territory and females.

Snow leopard

Leopards often live close to towns and villages.

Are white tigers and Siberian tigers extinct?
Nearly. The Siberian tiger is paler than most other tigers, but still orange-brown in color. Truly white tigers are extremely rare. They are not a distinct species of tiger, as any species can produce a white cub.

Which speedy animal is endangered?
The cheetah. It can run up to 62 mph (100 kph). It can't keep up its speed over a long distance, but runs this fast in short bursts. Both the African and Indian cheetah are endangered.

Where do big cats live?
Mostly in Africa, but also in Asia and the Americas. Both African and Asian lions are at risk. There are even some medium-sized cats in Europe – one is the European lynx, which is at risk from habitat erosion and hunting.

When did the first cats live?
The first known cats lived 35 million years ago. They were the ancestors of two feline families. One produced all today's cats (big and small), the other was the sabre-toothed family. The last sabre-toothed tiger died out several thousand years ago.

Which cats are the big cats?

Lions, tigers, cheetahs, leopards (including panthers), cougars (also called pumas), and jaguars are all big cats and animals from each group are endangered. There are also medium-sized cats, such as ocelots and lynxes, that are endangered. These are too big to be counted as wild cats, but too small to be called big cats. Both the Texas ocelot and the Spanish lynx are endangered.

How small is the smallest bat?

The smallest bat is the pipistrelle. They weigh between just 0.15 and 0.25 oz (4–7 g). From head to tail, they measure 1–2 in (35–45 mm), and their wingspan measures 7–11 in (190–260 mm). The Myanmar pipistrelle is on the "critical" list of endangered animals.

Are bats really blind?

No, they aren't. However, their hearing is more highly developed than their sight, as they rely mainly on sound for catching their food. As bats are mainly nocturnal (active at night), hearing is more important to them than seeing.

How many species of bat are there?

There are 951 species of bat, divided into 19 scientific families, and all of them are in danger of extinction. All these make up one scientific order, *Chiroptera*.

Where do bats live?

Bats can be found all over the world, in Asia, Australasia, the Americas, Africa, and Europe. The only places bats would not be found are at the Poles. They live in a variety of habitats, such as buildings, caves, and forests. They often spend the nights in towns, searching for food, but will usually return to their roost before dawn. Loss of habitat is one of the main reasons why so many bat species, such as the Seychelles seath-tailed bat, and the cusp-toothed flying fox from the Solomon Islands, are endangered.

When is a fox not a fox?

Flying fox

A FLYING FOX IS ACTUALLY A FRUIT BAT, A VEGETARIAN BAT THAT FEEDS mainly on fruit. Many fruit bats, such as Bulmer's fruit bat from Papua New Guinea, are endangered. One of these species, the colugo bat, is also known as the Philippine flying lemur. The largest flying fox's wingspan can measure up to 3 feet (1 m). Fruit bats live in warm parts of the world, such as Australia, Africa, the Pacific islands and Asia.

Is a bat really a bird?

No, unlike birds, bats are mammals, which means they have hair, or fur, and give birth to live young, rather than laying eggs. They also suckle their young, whereas baby birds are weaned from the moment they hatch. Bats are unique animals because they are the only mammals that can really fly.

How do bats find their way in the dark?

By using echolocation. This means that they make high-pitched sounds that echo from their surroundings. By listening to the echo, the bat can work out the shape and density of its surroundings and find food. Echolocation is also used by dolphins, porpoises, and whales.

Do vampires really exist?

Vampire bats are the only real vampires. There are three species of vampire bat, all of which live in South and Central America. These species feed on the blood of livestock, such as cattle, sheep, or pigs. Vampire bats are quite small and, although their bites leave distinctive marks, they don't usually kill the animals they feed on. But if the bat is carrying a disease, such as rabies, its bite can be fatal. Vampire bats are endangered because people are afraid of them, and tend to kill them as pests.

Horseshoe bat

The horseshoe bat has a horseshoe-shaped flap on its nose.

Why are bats endangered?

LIKE MANY OTHER CREATURES BATS, SUCH AS THE HORSHOE BAT, ARE threatened by developers and farmers who destroy their habitat. They are also in danger from the growing number of people who enjoy caving and potholing, and the common practice of cutting down old trees. Bats that live on fruit or insects, such as the Philippines tube-nosed fruit bat, are endangered by the use of pesticides.

The flying fox is so-called because it has a fox-like face.

How can people help bats?

Many people are frightened of bats. They feature in horror stories, because they are night creatures, and fly in a jagged way that can seem spooky. The best way of helping bats is to explain to people that they are harmless. Bats are very clean and do not attack people. People who realize that bats need friends sometimes put up bat boxes for them to nest in. These are like bird nesting boxes and they allow bats to roost and hibernate in peace.

Gray squirrel

Are rats related to squirrels?
Yes, they are both mammals, called rodents. The rodent family (scientific name *Rodentia*) includes rats, mice, dormice, beavers, porcupines, and squirrels. Many of them, such as the lesser-toothed small rat and the common fieldmouse, are endangered. They all have strong front teeth (incisors), which they use to slice through vegetation, such as strong grasses and tree bark – and beavers even saw through tree trunks. Like other mammals, rodents are warm-blooded and give birth to live young, which they feed with mother's milk.

How do beavers build dams?
Beavers can cut down trees by biting through the trunk. Then they gnaw them into pieces and drag the logs to the water to build a dam. They lay the logs across each other and stop up any gaps with stones and mud. Beavers are severely endangered due to logging in Canada and North America.

Most squirrels only live for one to two years.

Did gray squirrels kill off red squirrels ?

N O. THE RED SQUIRREL WAS THE ONLY SQUIRREL LIVING IN THE UK UNTIL the gray squirrel was brought in from the USA. When red squirrels started to disappear, many people thought gray squirrels were killing them. But now scientists believe that the red squirrel was endangered by other predators, such as stoats, foxes and eagles. A highly contagious disease also killed vast numbers of red squirrels, in the first half of the 20th century. Gray squirrels are larger and more hardy than red squirrels, so have survived better.

Squirrels have very strong front paws for gripping their food.

Are badgers related to weasels?
Yes! Badgers are a member of the weasel family, and so are stoats. They are all mammals, but weasels and stoats are carnivorous, which means they eat only meat, whereas badgers are omnivorous, which means they eat plant food as well as meat. Badgers are protected by law because they were in danger of extinction in the mid-20th century, from badger baiting (where dogs are used to kill badgers for sport).

How sleepy are dormice?

Dormice are said to be very sleepy creatures, but in fact they don't sleep for long periods every day. Like many mammals (including squirrels and bears) they hibernate in winter. They go to sleep in October and wake up in April. They wake up from time to time in winter, to eat food that they have stored up during the summer months. Dormice are endangered by pollution and pesticides as well as development.

Which small mammals are endangered?

Many small mammals, such as beavers in the USA and the red squirrel in Europe, are endangered because their habitat is being destroyed by humans developing land for building and farming. Others, such as weasels, are poisoned by dangerous chemicals used in industry and farming.

Red squirrel

Otter

Otters bark and chirp to communicate.

Where do otters live?

IN EUROPE, ASIA, AND THE AMERICAS. OTTERS NEED UNPOLLUTED WATER and they live wherever the water is pure – in streams, canals, and lakes, in mountainous regions as well as in valleys. Many otters are endangered because habitat destruction has caused them to starve, or because they cannot find unpolluted water.

Are rabbits or hares endangered?

Most species of rabbits and hares breed, well, like rabbits, and are not endangered! But a few species, such as the omilteme cottontail rabbit from Mexico and the Sumatran short-eared rabbit from Asia, are endangered because people are destroying their habitat. In many countries, such as Australia, rabbits are killed as pests.

Are any small mammals already extinct?

Yes. Scientists have found fossilized remains of several small mammals that died out many centuries ago, such as the macaca (monkey-like) and the leithia (a dormouse-like animal). Unfortunately many more small mammals may die out because of the destruction of their habitat – particularly animals that live in the rainforests, which are being destroyed by large-scale farming.

What is the world's rarest bird?

BRAZIL'S SPIX MACAW. THERE IS ONLY ONE MALE LEFT IN THE WILD.

Almost as rare is New Zealand's kakapo, of which there are only a few pairs left. Endangered birds include several birds of prey, shot as pests by farmers, and exotic birds, such as the flightless notornis, hunted by traders.

Why are people the birds' worst enemies?

People destroy birds' habitat by cutting down forests and draining marshland. A bird can die if it swallows a fishing hook, or fishing line, or rubbish that could injure or choke it. People sometimes steal birds' eggs, but if they disturb or look in nests, parent birds will leave their chicks to die. Exotic birds, such as parrots, pheasants, hummingbirds, eagles, and birds of paradise, are trapped to be sold as pets and often die while being transported. They are also killed for their beautiful feathers, or to be stuffed.

How can we count the birds?

We can't! There are birds in every continent of the world, and it is impossible to say definitely how many species exist. Even today, scientists are constantly discovering new species.

Where do budgies come from?

Budgies, or budgerigars, are native to Australia, where flocks of them can be seen flying wild. Their name comes from an aboriginal word meaning colored bird. They are a member of the parakeet family – which also includes parrots, cockatiels, cockatoos and lorikeets. Most wild budgerigars are green and yellow and they are at risk from hunters who shoot them as pests, or capture them to sell to the pet trade.

Kakapo

The kakapo hides under tree roots and foliage during the day. At night it searches for food.

Do crop pesticides harm birds?

Yes. Birds that eat sprayed crops, such as budgerigars and lapwings, can die from poisoning. Farm chemicals also pollute rivers and marshes and destroy water birds, such as the Jamaica petrel and the crested ibis from Africa, and their habitat.

Which are the biggest and smallest birds of prey?

The Andean condor is the largest bird of prey, with a wingspan of more than 10 feet (3 m). The smallest birds of prey are pygmy falcons. Some are only 6 in (15 cm) long. Both of these birds are endangered by loss of habitat.

Californian condors

The Californian condor only lays one egg when it breeds and it doesn't breed until it is six years old.

Are any birds extinct?

Yes. Some – such as the *Archaeopteryx* – died out with the dinosaurs. Others have been hunted to extinction more recently. Perhaps the most famous extinct bird is the dodo, which lived on the island of Mauritius and was finally killed off by hungry sailors.

Which endangered bird has the largest wingspan?

The wedge-tailed eagle, which can be found in Australasia, has a wingspan of up to 6 feet (1.8 m). From head to foot, the wedge-tailed eagle can reach a height of just over 3 feet (1 m).

What is a bird of prey?

THIS GROUP OF BIRDS INCLUDES EAGLES, FALCONS, HAWKS, AND OWLS. WHERE as most birds exist on a diet of small insects, nuts, and seeds, a bird of prey eats other birds and animals. Birds of prey have sharp, flexible talons (claws), used for grabbing their prey and for killing it. They also have hooked beaks for tearing and ripping at flesh. Because they are such beautiful creatures they are often hunted, to be kept and trained as pets. The Californian condor is one huge bird of prey that is endangered.

Index

AB

arachnids 10, 11

badgers 28
bats 26—7
bears 13, 14—15, 29
beavers 28, 29
bees 14
beluga whales 16
birds 30—1
birds of paradise 30
birds of prey 31
black bears 14, 15
black rhinoceroses 20, 21
black-backed jackals 9
blue whales 17
bone cave harvestmen 11
brown bears 14, 15
budgerigars 30, 31
burying beetles 10
bushbabies 6
butterflies 10

CDE

cats 24—5
cetaceans 16, 17, 18
cheetahs 24, 25
clouded leopards 24
cockatiels 30
cockatoos 30
cockroaches 11
colobus monkeys 6
colugo bats 26
condors 31
coral 18
cougars 25
coyotes 9
crayfish 11
crested ibises 31
crickets 10
cusp-toothed flying foxes 26

dingoes 9
dodos 31
dogs 8, 9
dolphins 16, 17, 27
dormice 28, 29
dugongs 18

eagles 28, 30, 31
elephants 22—3

FG

falcons 31
fennec foxes 9
fish 14, 15, 16, 17, 18, 19
flying foxes 26
flying lemurs 26
foxes 8, 9, 28
fruit bats 26, 27

giant pandas 12—13, 15
golden lion tamarins 7
gorillas 4—5, 6, 7
great white sharks 18
green sea turtles 18
grizzly bears 14

HIJK

hammerhead sharks 18
hawks 31
horseshoe bats 27
howler monkeys 7
hummingbirds 30

ibises 31
insects 10—11, 14, 31

jackals 8, 9
jaguars 24, 25

kakapos 30
killer whales 17
kodiak bears 15
krill 17

LM

lapwings 31
lemurs 6
leopards 24, 25
lesser-toothed small rats 28
lion-tailed macaques 6
lions 24, 25
lynxes 25

macaws 30
manatees 18
marmosets 6, 7
monk seals 18, 19
monkeys 6—7
moths 10
mountain gorillas 4, 5, 7
mountain lions 24

NOPQ

narwhals 17
notornis 30

ocelots 24, 25
omilteme cottontail rabbits 29

orangutans 6
otters 29
owls 31

panthers 25
parakeets 30
parrots 30
petrels 31
pheasants 30
pipistrelles 26
polar bears 14, 15
porcupines 28
porpoises 16, 17, 27
praying mantises 10

RS

rats 28
red pandas 12
red wolves 8
redback spiders 11
rhinoceroses 20, 21
rodents 28

scorpions 11
sea cows 18
sea snakes 18
sea-horses 19
seals 17, 18, 19
sharks 16, 18
shrimps 11
snow leopards 24
snub-nosed monkeys 7
spectacled bears 14
sperm whales 17
spiders 10, 11
spix macaws 30
spruce-fir moss spiders 11
squirrels 28
stoats 28
sun bears 14

TUV

tamarins 7
tigers 24, 25
tube-nosed fruit bats 27
turtles 16, 18

vampire bats 27
vaquita porpoises 16

WXYZ

wasps 11, 14
weasels 28, 29
wedge-tailed eagles 31
whales 16, 17, 18, 27
white rhinoceroses 20, 21
white tigers 25
wolves 8, 9

32